Over

MW01483827

The Ultimate Cure Guide for How to Overcome Fear Forever

presentation of the information is without contract or any type of guarantee assurance.

The trademarks that are used are without any consent, and the publication of the trademark is without permission or backing by the trademark owner. All trademarks and brands within this book are for clarifying purposes only and are the owned by the owners themselves, not affiliated with this document.

Table Of Contents

Introduction

First off, I really want to thank you for downloading this book. The pages in this book were developed through years of experiences that I have gone through, as well as what has proven to work for others that I have talked to and have researched. I also want to congratulate you for taking the time to understand your own fears and how you can overcome them.

After experiencing many different types of fears throughout my life and struggling to overcome them, I decided that I wanted to write a short, detailed book to help other people who are in a similar situation as I was. I also wanted to help people understand how fears form and why we experience them, because many of us have friends or relatives who struggle with fears and we have trouble understanding what is going on in their heads.

I can guarantee that you will find this book useful if you make sure to implement what you learn in the following pages. The important thing is that you IMPLEMENT what you learn. Fears are not conquered overnight but the important thing to remember is that it is definitely possible for you to overcome them. What I am giving you is the information so that you can better understand your own mind and body, as well as some steps you will need to make that journey.

Every person will experience fear in his or her life. A small amount of fear within you can be helpful in stirring up some motivation when faced with frightening situations, but hanging on to it for too long and with no good reason, can be nothing short of crippling.

As you go through these pages, you'll get a better understanding of what fear really is, where it comes from, and you'll learn several ways that you can overcome it. We will dive into what is going on in your brain, how your body reacts to your triggers, how your early childhood can influence the rest of your life, as well as what work is required of you to get past the roadblocks that you have.

I recommend that you take notes while you are reading this short and concise book. This will ensure that you get the most out of the information in here. I want you to feel that you made a purchase that was worth your money and so that you can refer back to your notes even after you've finished reading. The notes will help you to pinpoint exactly what you need to implement, and by writing things down, you will be able to recall specific ways to handle certain situations when they arise.

Lastly, remember that everything in this book has been compiled through research, my own experiences, as well as the experiences of others, so feel free to question what you have read in this book. I encourage you to do your own research on the topics you want to look deeper into. The more you understand about your own mind and body, the better off you'll be. To overcome a fear in your life, it will take some work on your part, but you can do it! So remember to read with confidence and an open mind!

Chapter 1:

Understanding Fear

Each and every person, at some point, becomes afraid. People get scared of different things such as heights, death, driving, ghosts, being alone, and even a fear of the future. Fear is normal. It is a reaction or instinctual response when you feel like there may be a physical and emotional threat and/or danger coming your way. Fears are essential to our survival as a human race. Besides, you wouldn't be able to protect yourself from any kind of threat if you didn't feel the emotion of fear.

However, fears can become a problem when people fear circumstances that are far from any real danger and are just imaginary scenarios of the future playing out in their mind. Through years of research, we've learned that there are certain experiences, sometimes called traumas, which can happen in a person's life to generate a fear response much later in that person's life.

Pinpointing these events can range from being very obvious to extremely difficult. The good news is that the way to overcome these fear responses is within our own power. It comes down to pinpointing the events and then slowly exposing yourself to similar situations. This is often what psychologists, psychiatrists, and psychotherapists do when you visit them.

Scientists have also learned that fear of the unknown is a natural and basic human emotion that is meant to keep us safe as individuals and as a species. For example, historically, you would benefit greatly from having the fear of being lost in an unknown village. This kind of a fear would help us hundreds and thousands of years ago because societies were much less safe and had little to no connection to one another.

If you got lost back then, you might not be able to communicate with the other societies because of a language barrier or even worse, you may die of a disease because you are not immune to the diseases of this mysterious village. However, our world is much more connected today, and now that we're in a time where almost everything can be tracked or translated between cultures, this fear of being lost in an unknown village may still be there, but it has no real benefit to us anymore. In our current world, you can go into most countries and as long as you have some form of currency, you can survive.

Another example of this would be the fear of approaching a member of the opposite sex that we are interested in. This one here often holds many people back from living the kind of life they want. It is important to remember that when we lived in much smaller societies of 50-100 members, it would benefit us to have a fear of approaching an unknown member of the opposite sex because we could be risking our safety or even our chance of reproducing. In those days it was very important to be aware of these things because inbreeding and social hierarchies were key to our individual survival, as well as the survival of our tribe.

This also had a huge impact on our social status, if we were to mess up with a certain member of the opposite sex that we were interested in. Could you imagine how the other members of the opposite sex would judge you if you developed a bad reputation with another? All of your potential mates could reject you, just because you made a few mistakes or were not mature enough at the time. But in the world we live in today, you could live in New York City and not see someone you dated for months or years!!

So how does that fear of approaching the opposite sex benefit us in today's society? It doesn't. In fact, as long as you are respectful to that person and the environment you are in, you can approach whoever you are interested in with really no consequences at all! So this fear doesn't really have a use in our current overcrowded society. Unfortunately, many people haven't been able to live fulfilling dating lives because they allow their fear of approaching a member of the opposite sex to override their own desires of happiness.

Depending on your point of view, you may consider these kinds of fears as a hindrance towards your own personal growth. As a human being, you will undoubtedly begin to feel fear at times, but you have to be cautious not to allow it to negatively influence any of your actions or decisions in life. Unfounded fear can usually jeopardize your chances of success, for it can be a controlling and manipulating factor in life.

Fear can also be deemed "real" or "imaginary" and is felt due to the interpretation of a situation. It can make you feel anxious and pessimistic and incapable of thinking rationally. You'll tend to procrastinate or become doubtful and let it set some limitations in terms of your own abilities. It is also important to note, two different individuals can view the same situation completely differently.

If person A and person B have both never been in a plane before, they are both completely new to the phenomena of flying on a plane. However, if person A views the action of flying in a plane to be a new experience that will expand their view of the world and person B views this action as an extremely risky situation that he/she should avoid because of the movies they've seen, person A will feel little to no fear when the plane is starting up while person B could be terrified the entire trip. By keeping this in mind, you will be more in control of how you feel in a new or different situation.

One key is to never let your mind settle on negative thoughts that can lead to fear. Instead, fill it with courageous thoughts and your fears will eventually fade away. Courage is not really the absence of fear, but instead it is being able to prevail over the fears that are there. If you allow your mind to keep on anticipating that something horrible is bound to happen, your mind will only be clouded with daunting thoughts. The same can be said with positive thoughts.

The Brain Involvement

The human brain is an extremely complex organ. The nerve cells consist of a network of communications where everything you think, feel, and do starts. Some of these create involuntary responses, which includes the fear response. You don't intentionally activate it or know that it's happening until it's already running its course.

Based on the studies that have been conducted in neuroscience, because the brain cells are continuously transporting information and generating responses, certain peripheral areas of the brain may be involved in triggering fear, and several parts of the brain play vital roles during this process.

We know that the thalamus is the part of our brain that decides where the incoming sensory data must be sent, and the sensory cortex is what interprets that data. The hippocampus saves and retrieves conscious memories and triggers the fight-or-flight response within our bodies. The amygdala is responsible for decoding emotions, determining potential threats, and storing memories of fear.

I know these terms may be complex for some readers and I don't want to get into too much detail about the scientific terms and definitions here because I want to keep this book as practical as possible. However, I do recommend that you look up more details about the information regarding the way the brain interprets and processes, especially in regards to fear.

The best part is that neuroscience is still a relatively new field within the sciences, and we are learning more and more about how the human brain functions each day. A couple hundred years ago, we didn't even know a fraction of the information that we do now, in regards to brain health and functionality.

Forming of Fear

The process of producing fear occurs in the brain while we are completely unaware. It starts with the terrifying stimulus that we feel and then ends with a fight-or-flight response. There are actually two paths concerning a fear response, which happen simultaneously: the low road and the high road.

The low road is rather sudden and chaotic, initiating several physiological changes including the acceleration of one's heart rate, increasing one's breathing rate and muscle tension - which can be summed up as the fight-or-flight response. This all occurs before the stimulus is identified.

The high road is more thoughtful. It takes more time in considering all options and provides a more accurate interpretation of what is really going on. It determines whether a perceived threat is real or not. It takes a little longer compared to the low road, which is the reason why unanticipated events such as knocking on

the front door initially cause immediate fear,
before a rational calmness settles in.

Identifying Fear

Fear isn't always considered as adaptive. A small amount of fear can serve as a motivation or encouragement in nerve-wrecking situations. It can help to sharpen the mind. On the other hand, there are several types of extreme fears that can be paralyzing or make one want to escape a situation, even when it is not the appropriate thing to do.

Once fear becomes uncontrollable, it can seriously affect a person's daily functioning. It is no longer adaptive if a person is constantly afraid of the things that haven't even occurred yet. Anxiety and panic are often the terms associated with these types of uncontrollable fears. They can have negative effects on a person's social and personal well-being.

Anxiety is a future-oriented fear. It is basically characterized by uneasiness in the mind and body, because the person doesn't have any idea of what could happen next. A person who suffers from serious anxiety attacks, struggles with the fact that they know they don't have any control over the upcoming events. To others, the fear of not having control over the future may seem silly, but it is important to understand where a person like this is coming from.

Panic is an abrupt physical response that a person experiences when there's actually nothing to be scared of. This kind of fear is often associated with phobia that can affect one's physical and emotional well-being. During a "panic attack", the person suffering may go through all kinds of physical reactions, such as shaking, grinding of the teeth, or even tapping. Again, this may seem silly to an outsider but it is important to remember that the person suffering from a "panic attack" is literally experiencing something completely different than a "common fear".

Why Do People Fear?

One thing is for sure, if people were not afraid of anything, they wouldn't live long. They would be careless when crossing a street, careless with poisonous snakes, and may even try to freely jump off of a tall building.

Generally, fear promotes survival, and this is how we've developed so much as a species. We try things and if there is a negative result, we learn to alter our behavior or avoid that activity completely. A perfect example of this is when a small child burns his hand on a hot stove and learns to never touch it again - based on his own experience.

Have you ever wondered why people make faces when they feel terrified? Some people say that this is a way to let other people know you are afraid when you don't speak the same language as them. According to Charles Darwin, it's a result of the intuitive tensing up of muscles caused by a developed response to fear. He stated that his reason and will were defenseless against the thought of a danger that he had never experienced.

Although most people are no longer fighting to survive in the wild, fear is definitely far from being an obsolete instinct. While the media and technology in the world have helped us to develop as a species, it has also caused many fears within our culture. Many modern humans tend to anticipate dreadful things that may possibly happen to them, which they might have seen on television, read in a magazine or online publication, or heard from others on social media. However, often times these are events which will not happen to the person or are very unlikely to happen.

Trained Fear

During the 1920s, John Watson, a psychologist, trained an infant to be terrified of white rats. At first, the little boy wasn't afraid of the animals and showed delight towards them. Watson taught him to fear the white rats using the Pavlovian conditioning in which they paired the stimulus, which was the rat, with a depressing effect.

Whenever the child tried reaching for the rats, the conductors produced an awfully loud nose behind the child. Because of this repeated event, the boy quickly learned to be scared of the animals. He started to cry and move away whenever he'd see, not just a white rat, but other furry animals as well.

Just like the little boy's fear of white rats, the fear of normal pet dogs is also probably a conditioned reaction. Some people literally consider dogs as part of their family, while there are others who fear dogs as much as they'd fear a large monster. A large dog may have bitten a person when he/she was a small child, and the brain still associates the sight of a dog with the pain of being bitten.

You also may have been raised in a family where dogs were forbidden or maybe you were told to never pet a dog because it may bite. This type of conditioning is usually carried with a person until their late teens or early-20s, when they often start to question these long-held beliefs. For many people, this is the point where they start to develop their own world view, where they may come into contact with their fear (dogs) or things associated with their fears (dog owners) and begin to notice an inconsistency with their fears and what their logic is telling them.

Basically, fears from childhood are usually carried into adulthood. Common fears from a person's childhood include small insects, bigger pets, disappointing their parents and other family members, as well as public speaking, or even going to the dentist.

Chapter 2:

Causes of Fear

There are several factors that can play an important role when it comes to causing fear in our personal experiences of the world. A person may have suffered from anxiety, fears, or phobias during their childhood, went through an intensely stressful or rough time, experienced a painful or traumatic event, or a combination of any of these occurrences.

It is important to know that a person's memory is considered qualitative and not quantitative. It assigns a different amount of power to each and every memory. For instance, you may have already driven a car thousands of times without encountering any kind of problem at all, and then suddenly, you get into an accident and become scared of operating a vehicle henceforth.

Now, that one experience actually "weighs" more in your mind than the other thousand occurrences of problem-free driving. This is where it is important to use your logic and not give into the emotion of irrational fear.

Some studies regarding the areas of the brain that are affected in connection to fear, anticipated that a person learns to be terrified of something whether they personally experience trauma or merely observed the fear based on other people's responses.

This is very important because it tells us that our fears can develop based on the influences that we choose to put into our brains. This can be through reading something with negative content, seeing something negative, or listening to something negative. Basically, the key here is that you will begin to fear things that someone else is telling you to fear, whether or not you would actually think that based on your own experiences. When it comes to mass media, the common term that people use to describe this is "fear mongering".

The possibility of pain from an unknown event can also cause fear. The amygdala detects this potential and then transmits the signal, which creates the fear emotion. Emotions set off various instinctual behaviors and attitudes, unlike the logical brain.

The limbic brain selects a specific emotion to deal with a particularly challenging incident in life. While anger takes action in supporting an argument, fear answers to threats by recalling terrifying images, making the body ready for flight, and by means of gesturing the muscles to either freeze or flee.

Low-road fear acts almost instantaneously. Before you can even try walking towards the edge of a cliff, your muscles will immediately stiffen. Fear signals your body to work quickly to evade danger, but they tend to intensify once the danger becomes inevitable. They slow down conscious thinking and begin subconscious searches for some type of escape route, while the body prepares ways to protect itself.

Images of certain outcomes of failure will start to flash, and the fear emotion intensifies when there is a lack of opportunity to escape. This can sometimes be considered as a "life or death" situation, where the body and mind are realizing that a person must use everything he/she has, in order to escape the current life threatening situation.

At this point, amazing feats can occur. There is a term called "hysterical strength", which describes displays of extreme strength by humans, beyond what is believed to be normal. Hysterical strength is a term that people use to describe events like when a mother is able to lift a car up because her newborn son is trapped underneath. She may never be able to lift that car up on a normal day, but because of the circumstances at hand, her body and mind is able to conjure up enough strength to make it happen, because of how much that situation means to her.

You can find many examples of these cases on the Internet if you search for "hysterical strength" on Wikipedia. These events can only happen in life or death situations. On a smaller scale, you may have even noticed in yourself that whenever you have extremely stressful or scary situations in your own life, you can come up with the most brilliant ideas or run faster than you ever thought you could. You may even notice that you would not be able to achieve such feats if you were in a calmer, relaxed state of mind. This is because your brain and body is in such an altered state that you literally think and act differently than you can in a state of calmness.

Historical experiences and cultural influences also affect the formation of fear, especially after a severe accident has happened or during a person's childhood. As a child continues to grow older, fears suddenly start to pop into his/her head, which were never really considered an issue before. Most children, aged 2 or older, have already experienced being scolded, injured, or lost.

Fear of separation, particularly from parents, is one of the major fears in children, but this fearfulness will eventually subside as they start spending more time with other people. Fear of the dark is generally the hardest and largest fears to overcome in children. When they experience fears or phobias, they feel that these threats are real and parents would often have a hard time reassuring or consoling their child that they are safe and that there is nothing to fear.

Even though these types of fears are learned, it's part of a person's nature to fear. As a matter of fact, several studies found out that there are certain fears, such as fear of heights or potentially dangerous animals like snakes or lions, which are much more common than other types of fears like the fear of clowns, for example.

Chapter 3:

Signs And Symptoms

At birth, people are not conditioned to be fearful of certain things. This is apparent during the childhood stages. Children are naturally open and unrestrained. They're not scared of falling while they're learning how to walk because if they were, we wouldn't have anybody walking around today. After falling down repeatedly, it is only then that they are able to learn how to step one foot after the other.

It's when they grow older and begin to interact with different kinds of people that all these different feelings of fear are infused into them. Different influences like parents, peers, authority figures, and media influences all play a part in this. Some fears can last throughout one's entire life because of childhood conditioning, unless the person can first realize that the fear exists and then finds the courage to take action in order to completely overcome it.

Worry is another sign of fear. It is brought about by doubt in relation to something that normally leads to uncertainty or indecisiveness. It is also a kind of fear that involves a dreadful feeling of waiting for something to go wrong, although most of the time it will not even happen at all. This can be very dangerous to your success in life, because by definition, you are not living in the present moment, but always thinking ahead instead. Of course, the present moment is really all that any person has to actually take action.

There are other physical, psychological, and behavioral symptoms that may surface when a person fears something. We'll now go over what these symptoms are:

Physical Symptoms

Fear can trigger various symptoms that can directly affect several parts of the body. Headaches, exhaustion, muscle tension, chronic pain, restlessness, and stomach problems, including diarrhea and nausea are some of the physical symptoms that you may feel when fearful in a situation.

Dizziness or numbness, sweating, heart palpitations, shaking, choking or suffocating may also be experienced. It is important to remember that not everyone experiences signs of fear in the same way, but we all experience it in some way. The next time you are feeling some or all of these physical symptoms, pay attention to if you are also feeling fearful of something that is going on. You may be able to put these signs together.

Psychological Symptoms

There are many psychological symptoms that are associated with fear, such as irritability, nervousness, excessive worrying about uncontrollable events, increased self-consciousness, and failure to relax or concentrate. People who are experiencing anxiety disorder tend to have unrelenting, unfounded fears including fear of passing out, fear of death or doom, or fear of losing control in public.

These psychological symptoms often accompany the physical symptoms that were listed previously. Become conscious of these symptoms when you are experiencing a fear response as it can help you to take control of the situation you are in without letting the fear become too strong.

Behavioral Symptoms

Usually when a person feels fear, behavioral symptoms may show up. These can include sleep and appetite disturbances, absentmindedness, social withdrawal, avoidance, clinging to reminders, or even crying. It is important to be aware of these behavioral symptoms in yourself when trying to pinpoint the cause of your fears.

Behavioral symptoms are often the symptoms that can be the most dangerous, as far as your personal successes. It can limit your interactions with others and can affect your family life. Be sure to notice these symptoms as early as possible so that you may stop them from reoccuring. You never want behavioral symptoms to take over your daily activities because before you know it, you may lose control of your emotional well-being.

Panic Attacks

Panic attacks are primarily associated with panic disorder. It is the sudden, unexpected onset of physical and psychological symptoms of anxiety or fear. It may last for about 5 to 30 minutes. panic attacks that are untreated may result in the development of certain phobias. Shortness of breath, increased heart rate, chest pain, sweating, and disease are some of the physical symptoms of panic attacks. It can make a person feel disassociated and create a feeling of insanity.

If you are experiencing something that seems like a panic attack, it is important to see a professional who can better judge the situation. You never know if what you think could be a panic attack is actually something different like a heart palpitation or an issue with your lungs. Make sure to be aware of the symptoms!

Chapter 4:

Ways to Overcome Fear

Fear is often considered by many in the self-help industry to be the enemy of success. Great rewards are obtained from taking risks in life. If fear often reigns within you, you'll never have the courage to take risks and you'd have a very difficult time accomplishing anything great.

Experiencing natural fear from time to time is part of life. It is a normal thing, but it can be physically and emotionally weakening if you live with constant fear. You won't be able to live your life to the fullest if you keep on refusing to join various daily activities just because you might have to face your fear of social interaction.

Even the bravest people in the world have certain fears that they have had to overcome. It doesn't really matter whether you're afraid of heights, spiders, failure, or change as long as you're courageous enough to accept, confront, and take control of your fears to keep them from restraining you, when it comes to the things you want to do most in your life.

Sooner or later, you may start to unconsciously acquire new fears, but you shouldn't dwell on them and make it a priority to unlearn those new fears as well. It's important not to deny having such fears and being aware of them is also essential, as you begin the first step towards eradicating them. Anyone can learn how to overcome fear. It's a skill. People usually just cling to them because their fears are a part of their entire disposition. There's nothing wrong if you feel like you're not yet ready to face your fears, but you will know when it is the right time. Once you've decided to start conquering your fears, here that the things that will help you accomplish your goals:

Analyze & Evaluate Your Fears

Acknowledge It

Ignoring or denying the fact that you have fears, even to yourself, is a very easy thing to do, especially when you want to appear brave or strong to others. The truth is, you can't really consider yourself as brave if you aren't able to accept the fact that you have fears in the first place.

Acknowledging your feelings is the first step in taking control over the situation. Write down on a sheet of paper, "I (insert name), am currently afraid of (insert fear) and I will overcome this fear because I want to accomplish..... "

Identify Your Fears

Sometimes fear can be easily recognized, but other times you can't even explain where those anxious feelings are coming from. Learn to name your fears. What is it exactly that makes you so afraid? Once you understand what your fears are about, you're already on your way towards eliminating them.

Journaling can be a good way to keep track of your progress while you're striving to overcome your fears. Write down every fear that bothers you. Often times when I would write down the fears that I had, I started to realize that these fears only existed in my head and the chance of the occurrence actually happening in reality was slim to none.

Identify the Structure

Dealing with your fear and considering it as something that has a beginning and an end can surely help you realize that you have control over it. Delve into it's roots. When, where, and how did it begin? Did it start with a traumatic experience? Does it have anything to do with your childhood environment at school or home? How long have you been afraid of said thing? What triggers it and how does it affect you?

Fear is sometimes a healthy emotion that can protect you from harm or doing something silly. Find out whether you have a really good, realistic reason to possess this fear or if it is simply inhibiting.

Imagine Your Desired Outcome

As soon as you understand and recognize your fear, think about the things you want to change. Your main goal might be to overcome all of your limiting fears in life, but keep in mind that it is important to establish smaller, measurable goals to achieve success in the long-term.

Do it one step at a time. Imagine the person that you will be once you overcome the issues that you have right now, and think about how beneficial it will be once you get there.

Take Charge Of Your Fears

Gradually Lessen Sensitivity

Usually, people are afraid of things because they haven't correctly been exposed to them. We commonly describe it as "fear of the unknown". Try to expose yourself, little by little, to the things that you're afraid of, until you learn to understand them better and your fear of them will start to dissolve.

Here is an example that you can apply to your own situation:

If you're scared of spiders, start by taking a peek at some drawings of spiders until you learn how to manage your reaction from this activity. You'll be able to notice when your body has a less visceral reaction to the drawings over time.

Eventually, you can start looking at photos of real spiders. Again, notice the feelings that arise within you at the start of this process and then see how you feel after about a week of seeing a photo of a real spider every day. If you find yourself too afraid of the change, you can simply start by gradually altering your daily routine until you find yourself capable of handling whatever life throws at you. This pattern of continually exposing yourself to slightly more fearful stimuli is often called "exposure therapy".

It is important to remember that this practice can be applied to anything that you are scared of. After you've written down your fears and admitted to being afraid of those things, you need to focus on exactly what you CAN stand. What is it that you can tolerate right now?

Do that thing. Take the little step that is in front of you right now. Tomorrow's step will be for tomorrow. As long as you expose yourself to increasingly more on a daily, weekly, or monthly basis, you're on the right track.

I want you to imagine that you are climbing a staircase and you are at the bottom right now, while the vision you have of yourself is at the top step. Take a step each day, and before you know it you'll be approaching that top step.

Try Direct Confrontation

Sometimes, the best way to overcome your fears is to confront them, face to face. When you encounter the cause or basis of your fears, you might realize that there's really nothing to be afraid of and that you've just made up all those scary scenarios in your head.

Imagination can make reality look terrifying if it gets out of control. Once you've decided to take action, your fears become weaker and the new reality isn't as bad as you'd originally thought it would be.

Learn to Handle Failure

Facing your own fears can be quite difficult and challenging, and you don't always end up triumphant right away. You may have to face them many times before you can actually say that you've defeated your fears for good. You must make it a point to remember why you started on this journey in the first place.

Focus on how helpless you'll feel if you let the fear defeat you in the long run. This thought will help to drive you when times get tough. Remember that failure is only a stepping-stone on the road to your success. The world won't end when you fail at something, but your fear will stay scary if you quit and let it be that way for good.

Don't Stop the Momentum

Typically, dealing with fear involves a great amount of momentum. You may be reading this book after a build up of becoming frustrated with your fear. Likewise, you'll likely reach a point at which you'll be tempted to give up because of a few obstacles that you face.

Always remember that nothing is impossible when you're absolutely determined to achieve your goals. Perseverance is the key in getting past your fears. Don't worry about how much progress you made each day, just make sure that you are making progress over time. You should be trending upwards.

Let No One Stop You

There may be times when people will feed your fears and tell you that you're not good enough. Maybe they'll tell you that there's nothing you can do to change your current situation. Ignore these people and surround yourself with people who will boost your confidence and believe in your ability to overcome your challenges.

It is important to be open with others about what you are tying to overcome so that they can help you get through your struggles. It also helps to find someone who once feared what you currently fear and may have some strategies and/or tips that can be insightful for you.

Just as we mentioned earlier that negative influences can cause you to develop and maintain certain fears, the opposite is also true. You can influence yourself by listening, watching, and interacting with more positive people that encourage you. By doing so, you are stacking the odds in your favor and this is very important in regards to keeping your momentum going strong.

Change Your Perception About Fear

Turn Your Fear Into Attraction

The things that allow us to feel fear stimulates feelings of excitement and passion as well, which is why there are people who love horror movies or engaging in extreme sports. Try re-assessing your fear on a positive note and learn to appreciate the joy and pleasure that it can offer you.

Once you make it as your source of energy, you might eventually welcome it into your life with open arms. Look at it as a challenge in your life that you are going to overcome, something that you will look back on in 5, 10, or 20 years from now and say "I did that!". This will help you to be more optimistic in your abilities when you are struggling.

Consider Fear As An Opportunity

Fear can be a way to help identify and solve problems effectively. It serves as a guide that tells us when certain aspects of our lives need attention. When something unfamiliar scares you, consider it as a sign that you might actually need to know someone or something better than you currently do.

When you fear an upcoming deadline, see to it that you turn it into an opportunity to prepare yourself, whether it's writing a paper or delivering a speech. If you have a fear of water, think about all the possibilities laid out in front of you as soon as you overcome your fear. The thought of riding a boat or swimming and having a good time with your friends can be a form of motivation. When fear gets into your nerves, simply think of some happy or positive thoughts.

Provide A Rightful Place For Fear In Your Life

It's Okay To Be Afraid At Times

Fear is a natural emotion just like joy and sadness. Being fearful can actually help build one's character and teaches us how to become brave. You don't need to push or force yourself to overcome a fear just because you notice one of the earlier signs. If you notice that you are nervous to drive 115 miles/hour on the freeway, you shouldn't look at it as a "challenge" and make it your mission to overcome it.

Remember that if you notice a fear, any fear, come up in your life and you are wondering whether or not you should try to spend countless hours trying to overcome it, you can ask yourself an important question: "What kind of person will I become if I overcome this fear?" By answering this question, you will know if you should try to overcome it.

It is very important that you work on conquering the major obstacles in your life, but make sure that you don't strain yourself too much on things that don't result in any limitations to your daily life. The purpose of trying to overcome your fears is to free yourself to live a more positive life and to open up more doors of opportunity that you would not otherwise have.

Celebrate Your Triumphs

You don't have to wait until you've completely overcome your fear to celebrate. After you've set some small goals and made a few steps up that staircase, remember to reward yourself at every milestone you've hit. It could be something small, like when you saw a spider and didn't scream or travelled around the city all by yourself. When you realize and feel how good it is to conquer your fears, you're all set towards facing the next challenges in your life.

Seeking professional help is also a good way to overcome your fears, especially if your fears are affecting your personal happiness in multiple ways. A trained specialist can assist you in identifying the source of your fears and provide you with ways to cope with them. Sometimes people feel ashamed to see some type of therapist, but the real shame is living your whole life without taking any action. Don't ever feel ashamed if you are moving closer to your goals.

Conclusion

I worked hard on creating the best guide for "overcoming fear" that I could. Fears were stopping me from accomplishing many things in my life. After finally overcoming my major limitations, I wanted to give back to others. These are all the strategies and tips that have worked for me, as well as for others that I have talked to and researched. I guarantee that if you stay consistent, they will work for you as well. Be optimistic about your current situation and make small progress each day!

I really hope this book was able to help you to clearly understand fear and break it down so that it is less scary. If you feel like you learned something from this book, please send me a message letting me know your thoughts!

Thank you and good luck on your journey!

Made in the USA
Monee, IL
15 March 2023